CONQUER YOUR MIND

307 Affirmations to Create Confidence, Love, Wealth, Fulfillment, & Freedom to Finally Live the Life You Want

By A.C. Clint

As a show of appreciation to my readers, I've put together FREE resources, including **a inspirational music playlist booster to enhance the power of your affirmations**, and a **complimentary chapter** download on **attracting the success** you seek.

Click HERE to receive your FREE resources, and enjoy listening to your new music playlist.

Introduction

1. Optimism, Pessimism, & The Power of Your Story
2. How Affirmations Work for Celebrity Power-Players
3. Creating Happiness & Fulfillment
4. Secrets to Finding Serenity & Mindfulness
5. How to Think and Grow Wealth
6. The Leadership & Success Mindset
7. Thoughts for a Long and Healthy Life
8. Weight-Loss Mantras
9. Attracting Love, Self-Acceptance, & The Perfect Partner
10. 6 Keys to Creating Your Own Affirmations and Improved Self-Narrative

Conclusion

Speaking and Coaching

Introduction

"Your beliefs become your thoughts,

Your thoughts become your words,

Your words become your actions,

Your actions become your habits,

Your habits become your values,

Your values become your destiny."

- Ghandi

What would you be doing with your life right now

if you were madly, truly, deeply happy and

fulfilled? Just sit quietly for a moment with the question. Close your eyes and really think about it.

For years, I didn't realize happiness started from the inside out. I would chase wealth, lust, fame, Disney ideals of romance, and post Facebook photos of my eternal world travel quest for true fulfillment and acceptance. I was convinced that happiness was outside myself, just out of reach in the form of my 'soul mate', 'perfect job' or the 'million dollar business' that would finally slash open a hole in the fabric of the universe and lead to utter Nirvana. While chasing enlightenment, and looking in all the wrong places, I became exhausted. I'd sit and read and journal and dream, but I just couldn't figure out how to get from where I was to `there'.

Meanwhile, I constantly beat myself up for not having aligned the entire 'happiness' checklist and quota that life expected of me. Where were all the things those commercials and sitcoms promised I would have? Where was my hand-delivered package containing an attractive, loving spouse, 2.5 children, a three-bedroom house, a six-figure income, the career of Steve Jobs, the cooking skills of Martha Stewart, and a real life manifestation of my Pinterest dream board?

I had convinced myself that SOMEHOW, when all of these things aligned, I would truly become fulfilled. Instead of acknowledging the progress, success, and love that was already in my life, I measured myself against everyone else's Instagram filters and LinkedIn resumes. Instead of pausing to celebrate my accomplishments, I looked to the next step in the never-ending treadmill of elusive, and unattainable "happiness".

Naturally, striving for fulfillment that was just out of reach caused me to spiral into abusive self-talk. Perhaps you are familiar with a few of these insane inner-dialogues?

"Why aren't you as successful as everyone else? You are so far from achieving your goals. You're lacking a real career. You need to be more productive. Stop doing nothing and being lazy! We need more money but I don't know what kind of job I would like. I am late again. I need to be more organized and less sloppy. Why am I so stupid? I'm lazy and worthless. I will never change and I will be directionless and poor my whole life and will never be able to retire comfortably. I'm fat. I can't stop eating. I just need to be five pounds lighter. I should be married and have kids by now. Everyone else is more accomplished than I am. I don't have enough money. I'm not attractive enough. I'm not muscular enough. If I go after what I really want, I could fail and terrible things will happen. I'm afraid of being alone and broke. Everyone is judging me. I'm not as smart as other people. My co-workers hate me. Is my friend mad at me? I'm not good enough for the person I want to be with. I'm suck at math. If I say what I really think, I'll embarrass myself. I better do what I'm told so no one gets mad."

Not too long ago, I was being run into the ground by this type of monologue. I had (almost) everything my inner slave driver ever wanted. I didn't realize the 'happiness' I sought, was only a mirage thrust upon me.

Leading a 'perfect' life is actually a hell of a lot of work. Keeping up a drool-worthy social media collage required I bend and contort to constricting and heavy expectations from myself, everyone around me, and even from businesses selling things I didn't need, from people I didn't know. I felt defeated, trying to dress immaculately, stay the perfect weight, and adhere to my manager's changing whims and mood swings with a smile. It was so much work; I suddenly began to deeply pity the people around me with "successful" burdens like children and mortgages.

The truth is, I had it backwards. I thought I would be happy once I was successful. It turns out that *inner-happiness* is the secret key to creating success. This is becoming more evident in scientific-backed studies, including research from Harvard:

"If we can get somebody to raise their levels of optimism or deepen their social connection or raise happiness, turns out every single business and educational outcome we know how to test for improves dramatically. You can increase your success rates for the rest of your life and your happiness levels will flatline, but if you raise your level of happiness and deepen optimism it turns out every single one of your success rates rises dramatically compared to what it would have been at negative, neutral, or stressed...If we know the intelligence and technical skills of an employee, we can actually only predict about 25% of their job success. 75% of long-term job success is predicted not by intelligence and technical skills, which are normally how we hire, educate and train, but it's predicted by three other umbrella categories. It's optimism (which is the belief that your behavior matters in the midst of challenge), your social connection (whether or not you have depth and breadth in your social relationships), and the way that you perceive stress." - Shawn Achor, Bestselling author of The Happiness Advantage

Studies included in Achor's book also reveal that optimistic sales people outsell their pessimistic contemporaries by 19% in the first year, and 57% in year two. I include more scientifically backed benefits of optimism in Chapter 1, as well as a formula to stop seeing the glass half empty.

Naturally, as I barraged myself with toxic insults, my balancing beam act started to waiver. At first, it was anxiety fits that kept me up until 2 a.m. Just a hint of light or the sound of a pin drop would startle me awake, and press the 'Play' button of a stressed out, self-loathing mental movie.

Eventually, the anxieties melted into exhaustion, and then to depression, and finally despair. I went from insomniac, to lethargic, napping sloth. There were days I'd lie in bed, curtains closed, as the sun outside slid back and forth from night back to day. I'd reached my breaking point. I couldn't take it anymore. I was fed up and done with the misery, pain, angst, and abuse.

In that moment of desperation, I remembered the tools I had used to create a life of happiness in the first place. All the joy I had to thank for in my life hadn't come from flogging myself with impossible goals day in and out. Quite the opposite: all of the wonderful things I had manifested had come from a place of self-love, joy, and undying belief.

Somewhere along the way, I had lost the key that had opened all of life's doors for me. I had let the cynicism of my disgruntled co-workers rub off on me, and the "You're not good enough" dis-ease of consumer culture infect the deepest caves of my mind. I let the news convince me the apocalypse was coming. I let everyone else's noise drown out my own voice.

It was in this dark moment, I remembered the shining light of optimism that allowed me to bravely keep adventuring and reinventing myself, over and over again. I opened my journal, and wrote: "Each moment I am conscious, I vow to believe my dreams are possible, and treat myself as someone I love truly and deeply, through the thoughts, actions, and choices I make."

It was ridiculous. How could I love, praise, and think highly of others, but not treat myself with the same respect and kindness? Why was I spinning in circles to please everyone around me, while flushing my own joy down the tubes?

I wasn't sure how to find my way back. All I knew was that I'd made a vow. This wasn't just a commitment, a wish or a "nice-to-have". I was going to go all in. I would think of any and all wonderful compliments I could give myself, and lay in bed for hours, repeating it again and again. My mind would naturally wander, like a rat down a sewer drain. I would stop it each time, and go back to repeating, "I am wonderful. I am happy". I started at night before bed, then in the shower, and on my morning drive to work. While talking to someone, inside my head I would chant, "I am magical. I am happy. I am successful. Everyone loves me. I love everyone." I could tell these thoughts began radiating out of me, as people began to react to me with invigorated respect and admiration.

I didn't stop there. I thought of all of the wonderful things my soul truly wanted out of life. I dug into the deepest caverns of my true desires, and proclaimed them to be mine, with every fiber of my being. Some would say it was a lie, but I knew the real truth. These wonderful things were happening, but just not yet. They were coming for me, and I was ready. The world was abundant and wanted to give me everything I needed. Life was already mine, and I just had to grab it.

My state of mind grew lighter. I became healthier and more energetic. Things happened that were fantastically out of my reach, that I never could have dreamt of. It was as if life said, "Finally! You figured it out."

My tyrannical boss, oppressive job, and toxic friends melted away to make room for a wonderful people and a new life that fit like a glove. Like a snake that shed its skin, I glowed with health, joy, and radiance. Finally, my existence became something I truly wanted, instead of confining shackles.

Incredible people came into my life, opportunities arose, and difficult situations naturally resolved themselves. The only word I could find to describe what was happening was 'magic'. Through it all, I'd repeat my affirmations: "I am fulfilled. I am in love. I am focused and successful. I am healthy. I trust myself." In less than a month, I was in great shape, naturally happy, and my smile was contagious.

In all honesty, I didn't believe the words at first. How many of us would? It didn't really matter. I was doing it in the simplest way I could muster, by focusing on one thought again and again and again until it was etched in my skull. What if you don't believe the positive words you tell yourself? Don't worry, and don't overthink it.

Your role is to lay the foundation brick by brick, reinforcing neuron connections, commanding every cell in your body like a general to his soldiers, and slowly build pathways with each repetition. The mind and body will respond automatically, without a choice. On a fundamental, even primal level, these words slipped past my conscious into my unconscious, where magic began to sprout.

Right now you might be hearing a voice say "As if. You don't love yourself. Not truly. You're not worthy of love. You have a messy house, a bad credit score, thank you notes to send, projects to finish, things to put on eBay, laundry to fold. You haven't even cleared out your email inbox. Who are you to love yourself?"

You might think the idea of "fake it 'til you make it: is cliché or simple enough to be idiotic. But truth and power lies in simplicity. That's the beauty of this practice. It's simple, it's practical, and the results are far vaster than your imagination. After all, if you believed you were capable of true happiness, would you limit your life to what you previously thought possible? Hell no. You'd push beyond every limit to blow your own mind.

The voice in your head will tell you that if you just do one more errand, or buy one more appliance, everything will be okay. This simple distraction seems so alluring, so you oblige. You strive to do one more thing, all the while worrying about the other things you haven't yet achieved. It's time to stop to and reflect. Are the things you're working your life away for reflect self-love, or just quiet desperation?

Think about the things that consume your life and your head. You have ONE life to live, and it's slipping away as you read. Don't spend it in an autopilot fog of living someone else's dreams.

Each day we are buried in a barrage of images and messages from media and society telling us who, what, and how we should be. We are led to believe that if we could only lead perfect lives, we would no longer feel inadequate. We perform, perfect, and please, all the while thinking, "What if I can't keep all of these balls in the air? When can I stop proving myself? What will people think if I fail or give up?"

"Perfectionism is just fear in really good shoes" – Elizabeth Gilbert

Use this book to engage your mind, heart, and spirit to wake up and think, "No matter what gets done and how much is left undone, I am enough", and to go to bed at night thinking, "Yes, I am sometimes afraid, but I am also brave. And, yes, I am imperfect and vulnerable, but that doesn't change the truth that I am worthy of love and belonging. I am a human *being*, not a human *doing*."

Remember that affirmations are a practice, just like meditation, exercise, or learning to ride a bike. You don't go to the gym once and consider yourself done. Believing in yourself and your dreams, perhaps, is the most important practice of all. To be successful, you must muster the same intensity you would use to pull yourself up if you were hanging off a cliff with one finger. As if your life depends on it. How would the next year of your life change if you believed in yourself madly, truly, deeply, and passionately?

There is one requirement: fierce commitment. This part can't be ignored. What if you don't believe that you can love or, even like yourself? It doesn't matter, so long as you remain open to the possibility.

As humans, most of our thoughts are re-living memories. We play familiar patterns in our head that trigger dreams, hopes, desires, and feelings like happiness, procrastination, or fear. These loops become so automatic; it feels like we are under their control, but that isn't the case.

Imagine a thought loop as a groove in the earth created by water. Given enough time, flow and intensity, and you will soon have a river. At first, a few words may have no power over you. Repeat them over and over, with passion, and your mental river will be unleashed.

The goal here is to create tracks deeper than the disempowering feelings laid down over previous years. You will notice shifts in your feelings, and beautiful occurrences in your life, until one day you'll love life, and life will love you back. It took me a few short months to go from misery to magic.

I can't quite explain it, but when you find yourself using the word "magical" to describe your life, you'll know what I'm talking about. Life loves to reward the grateful. Love yourself, and life will love you.

Once upon a time, I didn't understand why my success didn't feel like enough. I felt obligated to impress people or live a life that wasn't working. The direction of my life has changed dramatically since beginning an affirmation practice. The real me I'd hidden in fear of not being good enough, finally emerged.

I decided to try using the power of affirmations to manifest my deepest desires and deal with past traumas. Although skeptical at first, within months I experienced a profound self-love that radiated into my outer-life in the form of success, loving relationships, and meaningful purpose. It is mind-blowing what the power of thought can do.

In the end, I gave up everything I had and start fresh. I gave up my job, my apartment, and even my Tupperware. The new life I built is a much happier and more fulfilling one, free from the chains of self-doubt and fear. Safe to say, I love it more than ever.

Friends and family began asking me how I had rebuilt such joy and accomplishment so quickly, so I decided to analyze and replicate my process. I decided to publish the same affirmations that changed my life for others to use in difficult moments, to overcome fear and self-doubt, conquer big things, and live the life they imagined.

For what it's worth: it's never too late or too early to be whoever you want to be. There's no time limit. You can stop whenever you want. You can change or stay the same. There are no rules to this thing. We can make the best or the worst of it.

I hope you make the best of it. I hope you see things that startle you. I hope you feel things you never felt before. I hope you meet people with a different point of view. I hope you live a life you're proud of. If you find that you're not, I hope you **have the strength to start all over again.**

Always strive to be a better version of yourself. Don't remain stagnant, as your mind and your body will rot. Allow yourself to be creative, to chase your dreams, to open doors for yourself if nobody answers when you knock. I hope you use this book to do it. This experiment has been transformative for me, and I know it will be for you as well.

Chapter 1. Optimism, Pessimism, & The Power of Your Story

Do you feel stuck in negative thought patterns and frustrated by your lack of willpower? Do you know there is something more to life that feels just out of reach? Are you ready to obliterate obstacles keeping you from health, wealth, success, and fulfillment? Are you ready to create new experience and live the life you imagined? If you always stop before you even start, limiting beliefs may be holding you back.

If you want to live a better life, the clear answer to see the glass half full. Scientific research has come up with a long list of benefits to being optimistic and grateful. Research shows positive thoughts enable people to persevere and create more opportunities. Optimists are luckier. Research has also shown practicing gratitude causes (not just correlates with) an increased happiness levels. In fact, military training in optimism makes soldiers tougher and more persistent. Optimism can also create life benefits, because expectations often become reality. Expecting people to like you actually causes people to like you. Expecting a positive outcome from negotiations increased the chances both groups would come to an agreement they are content with. Optimism is also associated with a longer life and better health. Most people who live past 100 are happy, healthy optimists.

Some critics discard the validity of affirmations and positive narratives as a confirmation bias, defined as the tendency to search for, recall, and favor information in a way that confirms one's preexisting beliefs.

While this criticism may have some validity, it seems that confirmation bias actually creates tangible beneficial results for optimists and believers.

According to Dr. Jeremy Dean in *The Acceptance Prophecy:*

"Social optimists, of course, are in the happy position of expecting to be accepted and finding that, generally speaking, they are. Social pessimists, though, face the dark side of what sociologist Robert K. Merton—who coined the expression 'self-fulfilling prophecy'—has called a 'reign of error'. Expectation of rejection leads to the projection of colder, more defensive behavior towards others, and this leads to actual rejection."

There are benefits to pessimism as well. Pessimistic entrepreneurs are more likely to succeed. Optimists lose more money gambling. The best lawyers are pessimists, but also have higher rates of suicide, depression, and divorce. While pessimists may have a more realistic and accurate worldview, it's a lot of pain with less gain.

As Seligman explains in his book *Learned Optimism: How to Change Your Mind and Your Life*: "The defining characteristic of pessimists is that they tend to believe bad events will last a long time, will undermine everything they do, and are their own fault. The optimists, who are confronted with the same hard knocks of this world, think about misfortune in the opposite way. They tend to believe defeat is just a temporary setback, that its causes are confined to this one case. The optimists believe defeat is not their fault: Circumstances, bad luck, or other people brought it about. Such people are unfazed by defeat. Confronted by a bad situation, they perceive it as a challenge and try harder."

For example, pessimists tell themselves that when something bad happens:

1. **It will last a long time, or forever.** *"I'll never find love again."*

2. **It is universal.** *"ALL men are sexist pigs."*

3. **It is their fault.** *"I am terrible at playing slots!"*

In comparison, optimists, see the exact opposite:

1. **Bad things are temporary.** *"I'll have a new girlfriend again in no time!"*

2. **Bad things have a specific cause and aren't universal.** *"That job was toxic and not a match for me. The next one will be better."*

3. **It's not their fault.** *"I'm great at sales but today wasn't my lucky day."*

The ultimate difference between an optimistic or pessimistic, comes down to your self-narrative. **When bad things happen, what kind of story do you tell yourself?** Many psychologists believe that humans live inside the stories they tell themselves, and use those stories to define the world around them.

According to Psychology Professor Jordan Peterson:

"People who spend time writing carefully about themselves become happier, less anxious and depressed and physically healthier. They become more productive, persistent and engaged in life. This is because thinking about where you came from, who you are and where you are going helps you chart a simpler and more rewarding path through life,"

The goal of this book is to help you construct, craft, and augment the narrative you tell yourself. In the final chapter, I will dive even further into the art of optimism, and how to tell a self-narrative that will make you healthier, wealthier, tougher, luckier, and more well-liked.

Whether it's a healthy relationship, successful career, or healthy physique, I want to help you easily overcome self-doubt and take action to create a life you love. Are you ready to get started?

The key to creating the new experiences you want, is to clearly declare your desires. This book provides very clear positive statements about what you might want to experience in our world. Affirmations might seem too simple or good to be true, but you will rarely find a successful person who hasn't used the self-talk to succeed in one way or another. If repeated daily, the carefully constructed affirmations in this book will unlock hidden potential within you, and give you 3D vision to spot opportunities you never saw before.

On a personal note, I have used the power of affirmations to make a six figure income by the age of 25, travel to destinations including Bali and Greece, work on entertainment studio lots for Disney and the Simpsons, and just have better luck finding a parking space. While affirmations have helped me accomplish big things, more importantly, they help me find inner-peace and joy in my relationships and smallest daily interactions.

What are affirmations?

Affirmations are positive statement about something we want to create in our lives. An affirmation is really anything you say or think. Often, a lot of what we normally say or think is quite negative, and does not create good experiences for us.

If we want to change our lives, we have to retrain our thinking into positive patterns. Too often we say "I don't want this in my life", and forget to state clearly what we do want. "I don't want to be sick anymore" doesn't give your body a clear picture of the health you desire. Instead, try phrasing it as "I am healthy."

Why do affirmations work?

Research indicates self-affirming thoughts can lower our brain's stress hormone levels. The reticular activating system is a big name for a fairly small part of the brain that tells us what to pay attention to and what not to. Your RAS is responsible for 'confirmation bias' by taking what you focus on and creating a filter for it. It then sifts through data to present only pieces that are important to you. All of this happens without you noticing.

> **"Whether you believe you can do a thing or not, you are right."**
>
> - Henry Ford

The RAS seeks information that validates your beliefs. It filters the world through the guidelines you give it, and your beliefs shape those limitations. If you think you are bad at public speaking, you probably will be. If you believe you are efficient, you most likely are. The RAS helps you see what you want and therefore, influences your actions.

When you first say an affirmation, it will not seem to be true. If it were, you wouldn't need the affirmation. It might even feel a little uncomfortable at first. Remember that affirmations are like planting seeds. First they germinate, then sprout roots, and poke through the ground. It takes time to go from a seed to a tall oak tree, so be patient, and enjoy the ride.

Chapter 2: Celebrity Success with Affirmations

If you have any skepticism as to whether affirmations are the secret to changing your life and perception forever, or are simply new-age nonsense, perhaps these quotes from successful power players throughout the ages will offer you a more open perspective.

"Create the highest, grandest vision possible for your life, because you become what you believe." -Oprah

"The idea behind affirmations is that you simply write down your goals 15 times a day and somehow, as if by magic, coincidences start to build until you achieve your objective against all odds. An affirmation is a simple sentence such as "I Scott Adams will become a syndicated cartoonist." (That's one I actually used.) Prior to my Dilbert success, I used affirmations on a string of hugely unlikely goals that all materialized in ways that seemed miraculous. Some of the successes you can explain away by assuming I'm hugely talented and incredibly sexy, and therefore it is no surprise that I accomplished my goals despite seemingly long odds. I won't debate that interpretation because I like the way it sounds. But some of my goals involved neither hard work nor skill of any kind. I succeeded with those too, against all odds. Those are harder to explain, at least for me, since the most common explanation is that they are a delusion. I found my experience with affirmations fascinating and puzzling, and so I wrote about it. At this point, allow me to correct a mistake I made the first time that I described my experience with affirmations. If you only hear the objective facts, it sounds as if I believe in some sort of voodoo or magic. That's not the case. While I do think there is something wonderful and inexplicable about affirmations, I have no reason to conclude it is any more than a pleasant hallucination. But if it is a hallucination, it's a totally cool one. When I have flying dreams, I know they aren't real, but it doesn't stop me from enjoying the hell out of them. And so it might be the same with affirmations. Affirmations might be nothing more than a wonderful illusion that you can control your own luck. Skeptics have suggested – and reasonably so – that this is a classic case of selective memory. Perhaps I tried affirmations a bunch of times and only remember the times it seemed to work. That's exactly what I would assume if someone told me the stories I've told others. But working against this theory is the fact that affirmations leave a substantial paper trail. It would be hard to forget writing something 15 times a day for six months. And if it turns out that this is what happened to me, it's fascinating still, because it says a lot about how the mind works." - Scott Adams, *Dilbert* Cartoonist and Creator

"It's sort of like a mantra. You repeat it to yourself everyday. 'Music is my life, music is my life. The fame is inside of me, I'm going to make a number one record with number one hits.' And it's not yet, it's a lie. You're saying a lie over and over and over again, and then, one day the lie is true." - Lady GaGa

"Cherish your visions. Cherish your ideals. Cherish the music that stirs in your heart, the beauty that forms in your mind, the loveliness that drapes your purest thoughts, for out of them will grow all delightful conditions, all heavenly environment, of these, if you but remain true to them your world will at last be built... The soul attracts that which it secretly harbors, that which it loves, and also that which it fears. It reaches the height of its cherished aspirations. It falls to the level of its unchastened desires – and circumstances are the means by which the soul receives its own." - James Allan, *As a Man Thinketh*

"I am no longer cursed by poverty because I took possession of my own mind and that mind has yielded me every material thing I want, and much more than I need. But this power of mind is a universal one, available to the humblest person as it is to the greatest,"
- Andrew Carnegie

"It's the same process I used in bodybuilding: What you do is create a vision of who you want to be — and then live that picture as if it were already true." - Arnold Schwarzenegger

"The invisible forces are ever working for man who is always 'pulling the strings' himself, though he does not know it. Owing to the vibratory power of words, whatever man voices, he begins to attract."
- Florence Scovel Shinn, *The Game of Life*

"Well I mean positively and negatively, I mean you attract, I mean not just what you fear, you attract what you feel, what you are."

- Denzel Washington

"I would visualize having directors interested in me and people that I respected saying that 'I like your work'. . . I would visualize things coming to me that I wanted. . . I had nothing at that time, but it just made me feel better. At that time all it really was for me was making me feel better. I would drive home and think 'Well, I do have these things; they're out there and I just don't have a hold on them yet, but they're out there. I wrote myself a check for $10,000,000 for acting services rendered. I gave myself 3 years and I dated it Thanksgiving 1995. I put it in my wallet and I kept it there, and it deteriorated… But then, just before Thanksgiving 1995 I found out I was going to make $10,000,000 on Dumb and Dumber...This insane belief in my ability to manifest things… I think it's ultimately complete sanity, but I believe we're creators and I believe we create with every thought and every word. Every moment is pregnant with the next moment of your life. I believe in manifestation… You get it when you believe you have it and that's the key. People still sit around think 'when's it gonna come…' and that's the wrong way. You're facing the wrong way, you're facing away from it. You have to go 'it's here, it's here, it's here.'" - Jim Carrey

"Follow your bliss, and doors will open for you that you never knew existed. Follow your bliss and the universe will open doors for you where there were only walls." - Joseph Campbell

"Mind is the Master power that moulds and makes,
And Man is Mind, and evermore he takes
The tool of Thought, and, shaping what he wills,

Brings forth a thousand joys, a thousand ills: —
He thinks in secret, and it comes to pass:
Environment is but his looking-glass."

- Dhammapada

"We both believe, wholeheartedly, that our thoughts, our feelings, our dreams, our ideas are physical in the universe. That if we dream something, if we picture something, we commit ourselves to it and that it's a physical thrust towards realization that we can put into the universe. That the universe is not a thing that's going to push us around. That the world, and people, and situations are not things that are going to push us around. That we are going to… command and demand that the universe become what we want it to be." - Will Smith

If you were once skeptical, are you now ready to begin? In these affirmation sessions, you are going to experience deep changes in your unconscious mind, that will make achieving your perfect life feel effortless.

For best results, repeat your affirmations out loud every morning or evening. Find a place you won't be disturbed and let the words wash over you.

Chapter 3: Creating HAPPINESS & FULFILLMENT

I am attracting joy into my life.

I am deeply fulfilled with who I am.

This day brings me only joy.

I have everything I need.

Everything that the Universe offers, is already mine.

I am safe and sound. All is well.

Everything works out well for me.

I have the ability and smarts to get through anything.

I compare myself only to my highest self.

I am happy in my own skin and my own circumstances.

I am more than good enough.

I get better every day.

I fully approve of who I am, even as I get better.

Today is rich with opportunity and I open my heart to receive it.

I believe in myself.

I deserve the wonderful things that will happen to me today.

I love myself more every day.

I am blessed with an incredible family and wonderful friends.

I only engage in positive habits.

My attitude grows happier and healthier every single day.

I am always in the right place at the right time.

I have everything I need to overcome a challenge.

I learn and grow from every experience.

I am creating new successful & healthy habits.

My life is just beginning.

I am rich in health, wealth, and love.

I have the power to change and grow.

I'm allowed to do what I want with my life.

I am free.

I am making a difference in this world.

I am at peace with all that has happened, is happening, and will happen.

I only attract the best in my life.

I am at peace.

Today I choose to be happy.

My life overflows with happiness and love.

Opportunities and advantages come with every door that I open.

What I currently do is serving me towards my higher purpose.

My body is healthy.

My thoughts are filled with positivity

I acknowledge my own self-worth.

My confidence is soaring.

Everything that is happening now is happening for my ultimate good.

My dreams manifest into reality before my eyes.

I radiate beauty, charm, and grace.

I am understanding and compassionate.

I am calm and relaxed.

I can afford to take a nice vacation.

I trust myself and know my inner wisdom is my best guide.

I love and approve of myself.

I make the right choices every time.

I have integrity.

I am reliable and true to my word.

I feel secure.

Life is great.

I am proud of myself.

I am blessed with good luck.

I attract positive people in my life.

Chapter 4: SECRETS TO SERENITY & MINDFULNESS

My world is a peaceful, loving, and filled with joy.

I choose peace.

I surround myself with peaceful people.

My work environment is calm and peaceful.

I breathe in peace, I breathe out chaos.

My home is a peaceful sanctuary where I feel safe and happy.

I release past anger and hurt.

I fill myself with serenity and peaceful thoughts.

I send peace into the world.

I respond peacefully in all situations.

I wake up today with strength in my heart, and clarity in my mind.

My fears of tomorrow are simply melting away.

I am at peace with all that has happened, is happening, and will happen.

I am grounded in the experience of the present moment.

I am focused and engaged in the task at hand.

All is well right now.

I am grateful for this moment and find joy in it.

I gently and easily return to the present moment.

I observe my thoughts and actions without judging them.

I am fully present in all of my relationships.

I observe my emotions without getting attached to them.

I meditate easily without resistance or anxiety.

I release the past and live fully in the present moment.

Calmness washes over me with every deep breath I take.

Every day I am more and more at ease.

Being calm and relaxed energizes my whole being.

All the muscles in my body are releasing and relaxing.

All negativity and stress are evaporating from my body and my mind.

I breathe in relaxation. I breathe out stress.

All is well in my world.

I am calm, happy, and content.

A river of compassion washes away my anger and replaces it with love.

The more I give to the world, the more I get.

I have a heart of gold and share this with the world.

Following my intuition and my heart keeps me safe and sound.

I am grounded.

I draw from my inner strength and light.

I trust myself.

I trust my inner wisdom and intuition.

I breathe in calmness and breathe out nervousness.

This situation works out for my highest good.

Wonderful things unfold before me.

I forgive myself.

I let go of my anger so I can see clearly.

I kindly ask for help and guidance

I know my wisdom guides me to the right decision.

I receive all feedback with kindness.

I trust myself to make the best decision for me.

The past has no power over me.

I am a good person.

I love change and easily adjust myself to new situations.

I always attract only the best of circumstances.

All my problems have a solution.

I seek a new way of thinking about this situation.

The answer is right before me.

I am following the right path.

I live in the present and am confident of the future.

Chapter 5

Think and Grow WEALTH & ABUNDANCE

I love watching my money grow.

My income is continuously increasing.

I always have enough money to suit my needs.

I am generous with money as I know it will return in magnitude.

Money flows freely and abundantly to me.

I am rich.

I deserve to be paid well for my time, efforts, and ideas.

My life is plentiful with prosperity.

I am a money magnet.

I attract wealth and abundance.

I am easily able to provide for myself and loved ones.

My business is growing, expanding, and thriving.

I have lots of money in my bank account.

The universe is bringing me all the wealth I desire.

Every day in every way, I am becoming more and more wealthy.

I have an intention for wealth and know it is a reality awaiting my arrival.

I have now reached my goal and feel the excitement of my achievement.

I am fortunate.

Chapter 6: The LEADERSHIP & SUCCESS MINDSET

My potential to succeed is infinite.

I am fulfilling my potential.

I have wonderful work in a wonderful way.

I work very few hours for lots of pay.

I am indestructible.

I am courageous and I stand up for myself.

I am disciplined and productive in everything that I do.

I am successful in all of my endeavors.

Success is my natural state.

I easily find solutions to challenges and roadblocks, and move past them quickly.

Mistakes and setbacks are important learning opportunities.

Today I am successful. Tomorrow I am successful.

Every day I am successful.

I feel successful with my life right now, even as I work toward future success.

I know exactly what I need to do to achieve success.

I feel powerful, capable, confident, and energetic.

I have an intention for success and know it is a reality awaiting my arrival.

I have now reached my goal and feel the excitement of my achievement.

I think, act, and communicate like a leader.

I am an inspiration.

I am an effective communicator.

I am a role-model for others.

I inspire others to be their best self.

I lead by example.

Obstacles move out of my way with ease.

My path is carved towards greatness.

I am smart and intelligent.

I have lots of useful skills to offer.

I am blessed with skills and talents that the world needs.

I approach every situation with hope, courage, and optimism.

Creative energy surges through me and leads me to new and brilliant ideas.

I am achieving my vision of success.

I have a special talent for focusing in on the most successful opportunities.

I follow through on my projects to completion.

I have unlimited abilities to conquer my challenges.

When I breath, I inhale confidence and exhale fear.

I easily solve problems.

I always find the best solution.

I am self-reliant and persistent.

I am disciplined and organized.

I am energetic and enthusiastic.

I am creative and resourceful.

My confidence, self esteem, and inner wisdom increase each day.

My outer self is matched by my inner well being.

Anything is possible.

I travel in style for free.

World travel comes easily to me.

I fully accept myself.

I am worthy of great things in life.

Great things come to me every day.

I release and let go of worries that drain my energy.

I make smart, calculated plans for my future.

I show compassion in helping my loved ones understand my dreams.

I ask my loved ones to support my dreams.

I am doing work that I enjoy and find fulfilling.

I play a big role in my own career success.

I possess the qualities needed to be extremely successful.

I ask for and do meaningful and rewarding work.

My work impacts the world in a positive way.

I am able to change the world with the work that I do.

I follow through and reach my goals.

My dreams are unfolding exactly as I planned.

I am focused and on track.

The universe is bringing me everything I want very soon.

Chapter 7: Thoughts for a HEALTHY & LONG LIFE

I am youthful and energetic.

I am eternally young.

I am beautiful, inside and out.

I make healthy choices.

I take good care of my body.

My body is healthy.

I fill my mind with positive and nourishing thoughts.

My immune system is very strong.

Every cell in my body vibrates with energy and health.

I am completely pain free, and my body is full of energy.

I nourish my body with healthy food.

All of my body systems are functioning perfectly.

My body is healing, and I feel better every day.

I enjoy exercising my body and strengthening my muscles.

With every breath out, I release stress in my body.

I send love and healing to every organ of my body.

I breathe deeply.

I exercise regularly.

I drink lots of water.

I feed only good, nutritious food to my body.

I pay attention and listen to what my body needs for health.

I sleep soundly and peacefully.

I get lots of sleep.

I feel rested and energetic.

I am surrounded by people who encourage and support healthy choices.

I participate in only healthy habits.

I brush and floss my teeth every day.

I have lots of luxurious hair.

I have glowing, smooth skin.

I am happy, healthy, and vibrant.

Chapter 8: WEIGHT LOSS MANTRAS

My body is perfect.

Losing weight is easy for me.

I am the perfect weight.

My body is beautiful.

I exercise regularly.

I love getting my heart-pumping.

I only feed good, nutritious food to my body.

I love eating healthy, nutritious food.

I have released all attraction to starchy, sweet, and fried foods.

I feel energized by eating lots of fresh, colorful vegetables and lean protein.

I chose to eat foods that make me feel wonderful about myself.

My body knows exactly how much food I need to eat to be energized, healthy, and vibrant.

I know what I need to do to be slim.

Choices I've struggled with in the past are now easy for me.

Eating too much no longer appeals to me.

I love eating light and moderate portions.

I walk 10,000 steps every day.

Exercise makes me feel great.

It is a relief and a joy to be exercising regularly.

Exercise is fun for me now.

I look forward to moving and strengthening my body.

I look forward to stretching my body.

I love watching my muscles get stronger.

Exercise makes me feel exhilarated and energized.

I sleep soundly and deeply into the night.

I start my day with a healthy breakfast.

I like to eat early in the day, and avoid eating late at night.

I stop eating when I feel full.

My clothes fit perfectly.

I love how I look.

I feel confident and strong.

I feel powerful and in control.

I feel at peace with myself..

I am grateful for the body I have.

Chapter 9:

Attracting LOVE, SELF-ACCEPTANCE, & THE PERFECT PARTNER

I always see the good in others.

I forgive those who have harmed me in my past and peacefully detach from them.

I attract only positive, healthy people.

I am blessed with an incredible family and wonderful friends.

I love meeting new people.

I love my family.

My family loves me.

My parents love me.

The people I work with love me.

I show my family how much I love them.

I listen more than I speak.

My family is a gift.

I choose friends who accept and love me.

I surround myself with people who respect me and treat me well.

I take the time to show my friends that I care about them.

I am beautiful and smart, and that's how everyone sees me.

I never know what incredible person I will meet next.

I surround myself with positive and loving people.

I love myself as I am.

I attract people who love and accept me.

I bless the past with love, and let it go.

I am ready to be in love.

The perfect partner for me is coming into my life sooner than I expect.

I'm open to new relationships.

I accept my sexuality.

I'm ready to meet my perfect mate.

I love my partner with all my heart.

I am thankful to share this beautiful life with my partner.

My partner and I share a deep and powerful love for each other.

I respect and admire my partner.

I love my partner just as they are.

I love my partner's unique qualities.

My partner and I share emotional intimacy daily.

I have healthy boundaries with my partner.

My partner and I have fun together and find new ways to enjoy our time together.

My partner and I communicate openly.

I love sharing my life with someone.

I am responsible for my own happiness.

I resolve conflict peacefully and respectfully.

I am able to be completely authentic and myself in my relationship.

I communicate my desires and needs clearly and confidently with my partner.

I want the best for my partner.

I am passionately excited about my partner.

Being in a relationship is wonderful.

I am happily in love.

I attract love in everything that I do.

Chapter 10: Constructing Your Own Affirmations

Next time you are listening to the voice in your head chatter away, check yourself, and listen a little more closely. When things go wrong, your voice will tell a story. What explanatory style does it use? Are you blaming yourself? Making broad generalizations? Assuming the damage is permanent? That's pessimism. Are you blaming unique circumstances? Acknowledging this too shall pass? That's optimism.

Reciting positive dialogue and narratives doesn't mean you are lying to yourself. Reality is fluid, and a more negative perspective doesn't always mean a more accurate perspective. No one is 100% at fault and always gets things wrong, and almost nothing is permanent or all encompassing. In this way, a negative perspective can be even more false than a positive one.

Put on some rose-tinted glasses and become the victorious hero of your own life by making these adjustments to your world view:

1. Adjust permanent outcomes to temporary ones.
2. Acknowledge specific circumstances, instead of making broad, generalizations and assumptions.
3. Change self-blame to a perspective of shared responsibility.

If there are specific things you would like to accomplish, you can begin to create affirmations unique to your lifestyle and desires. Below is the step-by-step process you should consider to create what you desire as quickly as possible, and avoid any negative hazards or roadblocks.

- Start with the words "I am." Make affirmations for yourself, not others.
- Use the present tense. Declare what you want to be already true. If you write your affirmations in future tense, then you will always be waiting for what you want.
- State what you want, not what you don't. Our mind brings what we focus on, so if you focus on something you don't want, you are still directing focus towards it.
- Keep it brief or even make it rhyme, so that it will be more memorable.

- "Be careful what you wish for" has been said for a reason. Make sure to be *very* specific.
- Whenever possible, use dynamic words that elicit action or emotion.

Conclusion

I hope this little book of affirmations has the enormous and profound impact on your life. Remember to read your affirmations out loud daily in the mirror, if possible. You might feel shy at first, but the outcome will be worth it. I hope you enjoyed this small book to create big life changes.

To your success,

A.C. Clint

PS- If you enjoyed this book, please don't be shy to drop me a line, leave a review, or both. I love hearing success stories from my readers, and how this book has changed their lives. I also love feedback, and reviews are the lifeblood of Kindle books, so five star reviews are always welcome and greatly appreciated.

SPEAKING AND COACHING:

Imagine going far beyond the contents of this book and dramatically improving the way you interact with the world, and manifesting successful real life results and relationships from simple habits.

Are you interested in contacting A.C. Clint? She is available for:

- A success mindset workshop for your work place
- Speaking engagements on the power of thought
- And so much more . . .

A.C. Clint speaks around the world to help people improve their lives through the power of building successful real life results through thought design.

A.C. Clint is a recognized industry expert, best-selling author, and speaker. To invite A.C. to speak at your next event, or to inquire about coaching, get in touch directly through her website's contact at www.annalisc.com or email at info@annalisc.com.

Made in the USA
Middletown, DE
13 September 2018